Mix it

Mocktail Recipes – Virgin Cocktails to
Get the Party Rockin'

BY

Daniel Humphreys

License Notes

No part of this Book can be reproduced in any form or by any means including print, electronic, scanning or photocopying unless prior permission is granted by the author.

All ideas, suggestions and guidelines mentioned here are written for informative purposes. While the author has taken every possible step to ensure accuracy, all readers are advised to follow information at their own risk. The author cannot be held responsible for personal and/or commercial damages in case of misinterpreting and misunderstanding any part of this Book

Table of Contents

Introduction

Why not ditch the vodka, lose the rum and mix up a refreshing and creative virgin cocktail?

Often mocktails are a bit of an afterthought, but they can be as creative and pleasurable as their alcoholic cousins.

With forward planning and a great mocktail recipe book, you can learn how to make non-alcoholic mojitos, juleps, and daiquiris.

Lots of our recipes use fresh fruit and flowers and are sweetened with herb-infused syrups and flavored with crème de cacao and cocoa powder.

Whether you are catering for an elegant affair, preparing party punch for a large group or treating yourself to a tipple, then it's time to rock the mocktails!

Coffee, Chocolate, and Coconut

Choco Coco Club Soda

A dairy-free iced coffee mocktail

Servings: 1

Total Time: 5mins

Ingredients:

- 2 tbsp. chocolate syrup
- ¼ cup coconut milk
- Ice
- ¼ cup cold brew coffee
- 1 slice orange
- 3 ounces club soda (chilled)

Directions:

1. In a tall glass, add the chocolate syrup to the coconut milk and stir well until incorporated.

2. Add the ice, top with the cold brew coffee and stir.

3. Garnish with an orange slice and fill the glass to the top with the club soda.

Chocolate Banana Slushie

A frozen banana slushie mocktail is so easy to make and bound to be a firm family favorite.

Servings: 1

Total: 5mins

Ingredients:

- 1 frozen banana (chopped into chunks)
- 1 scoop frozen plain yogurt
- 1 scoop chocolate ice-cream
- 1 tbsp. chocolate syrup
- ½ cup crushed ice
- Chocolate shavings (to serve)
- Cherry (to garnish)

Directions:

1. Combine the first 4 ingredients in a food blender and blitz on high until silky smooth.

2. Place the crushed ice in a tall glass and pour the mixture over the top.

3. Scatter chocolate shavings on top and garnish with a cherry.

Chocolate Dream

A creamy, chocolate mocktail perfect for the designated driver.

Servings: 3

Total Time: 5mins

Ingredients:

- 7 ounces milk
- 8 squares (5¼ ounces) chocolate bar (divided)
- 2 ounces vanilla syrup

- 3 squares milk chocolate
- Ice

Directions:

1. In a small saucepan gently heat the milk.

2. Add 4 squares of chocolate to the milk and stir until the chocolate has combined and the ingredients are incorporated.

3. Set the chocolate mixture to one side to cool for 60 minutes, or until at room temperature. Transfer to the refrigerator.

4. Pour the cold mixture into a cocktail shaker and stir in the vanilla syrup.

5. Shake it all about for 60 seconds and double strain into 3 martini glasses.

6. Made a small cut in each of the remaining 4 squares of chocolate and place a square on the edge of each glass.

Chocolate Orange Mocktail

This mocktail taste just like the chocolate orange candy version.

Servings: 1

Total Time: 3mins

Ingredients:

- 4 ounces orange juice
- 2 ounces half and half
- ½ ounce crème de cacao
- Ice

Directions:

1. Add the orange juice, half and half and crème de cacao to a cocktail shaker.

2. Add a little ice and shake it all about.

3. Strain, serve and enjoy.

Coco Colada

A totally, tropical fruit combination made with pineapple and coconut.

Servings: 1

Total Time: 5mins

Ingredients:

- 4 ounces fresh pineapple juice
- 2 ounces cream of coconut
- 1 cup ice
- 1 orange slice

Directions:

1. Add pineapple juice, cream of coconut and ice to a food blender (suitable for ice) and process to a slush.

2. Add a drop of water if the mixture is too thick or a splash of pineapple juice if it's too thin.

3. Pour the mixture into a chilled hurricane style glass and garnish with a slice of fresh orange.

Coffee Mint Julep

Nothing says here comes summer like a Mint Julep, but fortunately, you can enjoy this mocktail version all year round

Servings: 1

Total Time: 3mins

Ingredients:

- 4 fresh mint leaves
- 3 ounces cold brew coffee concentrate
- 1 ounce simple syrup
- Crushed ice

Directions:

1. Taking care not to tear, muddle 4 fresh mint leaves in the bottom of a tall glass.

2. Add the coffee concentrate, simple syrup and fill to the top with ice.

3. Stir to combine.

Guava Coconut

The simplest of mocktails!

Servings: 1

Total Time: 2mins

Ingredients:

- Coconut water
- Guava nectar

Directions:

1. Fill a glass with equal quantities of coconut water and guava nectar and stir.

Iced Ginger Coffee

The caffeine buzz more than compensates for the lack of alcohol in this ginger-infused mocktail

Servings: 2

Total Time: 1hour 20mins

Ingredients:

Ginger syrup:

- 1 cup sugar
- 1 cup cold water
- 1 cup ginger (freshly grated)
- Ginger extract:
- 1 piece 3" fresh ginger (finely grated)

Creamy Coffee Mocktail:

- 2 shots freshly brewed espresso coffee
- 4 tbsp. ginger syrup
- 2 tsp fresh ginger extract
- ½ cup whole milk + extra for frothing
- Brown sugar (for rimming)
- Chocolate shavings (to serve)

Directions:

1. First, make the ginger syrup. Combine the sugar along with the cold water over medium heat until the sugar completely dissolves. Add the ginger and cook until a syrup consistency is achieved.

2. Using a sieve strain the syrup into a mason jar and place in the refrigerator for up to 7 days. Discard the grated ginger.

3. To make the extract of ginger finely grate a 3" piece of ginger, squeezing out the juice. Allow to stand for 4-5 minutes before you decant. Discard any white residue at the bottom.

4. In a mixing bowl, combine the freshly brewed coffee along with the ginger root extract and ginger infused syrup. Stir well to combine. Next, add the milk and transfer to the refrigerator to chill.

5. Heat the additional milk (for frothing) in the microwave and whip into a foam using an aerator.

6. Pour the mocktail into martini glasses. Spoon the frothy foam over the surface and garnish with chocolate shavings.

Key Lime Coconut 'Pie' Mocktail

With all the flavor of a good key lime pie with a punch of tropical coconut flavor, this is one delicious mocktail.

Servings: 1

Total Time: 2mins

Please make one of these for me!

Love

Mum

xxx

Ingredients:

- 3 ounces limeade
- 1 ounce canned coconut milk
- ½ tsp confectioner's sugar
- 1 ounce Key lime juice
- 2 drops vanilla essence
- 1 tsp flaked coconut (for garnish)

Directions:

1. Add all ingredients into a cocktail mixer along with ice. Shake well for 30-45 seconds and strain into a cocktail glass.

2. Sprinkle the coconut flakes on top and serve!

Mint Chocolate Mocktini

If you love mint choc chip ice cream, then this is the mocktini for you.

Servings: 1

Total Time: 2mins

Ingredients:

- Chocolate syrup
- ½ cup chocolate milk
- 1 cup mint-chocolate chip ice cream
- 3 ice cubes
- 1 candy cane

Directions:

1. Carefully coat the inside of a tall glass using the chocolate syrup.

2. In a blender, combine the chocolate milk along with the ice cream and 3 ice cubes.

3. Pour into the syrup coated glass.

4. Garnish with a stick of candy cane.

Spicy Chocolate Mocktini

Who needs alcohol when you make this spicy mocktini?

Servings: 4

Total Time: 7mins

Ingredients:

- ½ cup white sugar
- 2 tbsp. cocoa powder
- ¼ tsp cinnamon
- 1 cup cold water
- 2 cups unsweetened almond milk
- Lemon wedge

Directions:

1. In a small mixing bowl, add the sugar to the cocoa powder and stir until incorporated.

2. Transfer 2 tablespoons of the mixture to a small side plate and set to one side.

3. Place the remaining mixture along with the cinnamon and water in a saucepan and over medium heat bring to a gentle simmer while occasionally whisking. Continue to cook until the sugar is dissolved and remove from the heat and put to one side to cool.

4. Using a sharp knife make a cut in the wedge of lemon, and run the lemon around the rim of each of the 4 martini glasses. Dredge the rims in sugar to coat.

5. Pour approximately half of the now cooled syrup into a cocktail shaker. Add 1 cup of almond milk along with 1 ice cube and shake it all about.

6. Strain the chilled liquid into 2 martini glasses,

7. Repeat the process and serve garnished with a lemon wedge.

Strawberry Coconut Mocktails

A fruity, refreshing and fabulous mocktail for all the family to enjoy.

Servings: 2

Total Time: 5mins

Ingredients:

- 6 large strawberries
- ¼ cup fresh orange juice
- 1 cup coconut water

Directions:

1. In a food blender, process the strawberries along with the orange juice.

2. Evenly divide the mixture between 2 glasses and fill with coconut water.

Triple Chocolate Raspberry Mocktini

A decadent triple chocolate mocktini made with chocolate milk, cocoa powder and dark choc chips flavored with fresh raspberries.

Servings: 1

Total Time: 5mins

Ingredients:

- ½ cup raspberries (frozen)
- ⅔ cup chocolate flavored milk
- 1 tbsp. sweetened cocoa powder
- 1 tbsp. dark choc chips
- 1 fresh strawberry (for garnish)

Directions:

1. Add all ingredients into a blender. Blitz until smooth.

2. Serve in a martini glass and garnish the rim with a fresh strawberry.

Fruit

A Fuzzy Apricot

Apricot nectar, ginger ale, and lemon make for a classy and delicious alcohol-free tipple.

Servings: 1

Total Time: 5mins

Ingredients:

- Ice
- ⅓ cup canned apricot nectar
- Fresh wedges lemon
- Ginger ale

Directions:

1. Fill a tumbler glass with ice.

2. Pour in the apricot nectar, add the lemon wedges and fill the glass to the top with ginger ale.

3. Use a long spoon to stir the mocktail and serve.

Banana Tropicana

Transport yourself to a tropical white sand beach with this fruity banana, pineapple, and lemon flavored mocktail.

Servings: 1

Total Time: 5mins

Ingredients:

- 1 ripe banana (chopped)
- ¼ cup non-sparkling lemonade
- ½ cup pineapple juice
- 2 tsp white sugar
- ½ cup ice (crushed)

Directions:

1. Add the first 4 ingredients into a blender. Blitz until smooth.

2. Add the ice and pulse a few times until combined.

3. Pour into a cocktail glass and serve.

Classic Shirley Temple

A perfectly patriotic red, white and blue mocktail ideal for any 4th of July party or get together.

Servings: 8

Total Time: 5mins

Ingredients:

- Handful ice
- 8 ounces grenadine
- 2 liters lemon and flavored lime soda
- Maraschino cherries (for decoration)

Directions:

1. Add a generous amount of ice into each glass and pour over an ounce of grenadine.

2. Top each with 8 ounces of soda. Gently stir well with a long spoon.

3. Garnish each glass with 1-2 cherries and serve!

Fly the Flag Mocktail

A perfectly patriotic red, white and blue mocktail ideal for any 4th of July party or get together.

Servings: 1

Total Time: 10mins

Ingredients:

- ¼ cup fresh strawberries
- ¾ tsp grenadine
- 2 tbsp. sparkling water
- Handful ice (crushed)
- Lemon and lime flavored soda
- Fresh blueberries (for topping)

Directions:

1. Arrange the strawberries in the base of a tall glass and drizzle over the grenadine.

2. Slowly pour over the sparkling water and top with crushed ice.

3. Very carefully pour the lemon and lime soda over the ice so as not to disturb the grenadine too much.

4. Arrange a small handful of blueberries on top and serve!

French 75 Mocktail

Raise a glass to this invigorating mocktail.

Servings: 2

Total Time: 3mins

Ingredients:

- 3 ounces fresh lemon juice
- 4 dashes lemon bitters
- 2 (8 ounce) bottles premium tonic water
- 2 rock candy swizzle sticks

Directions:

1. Add the lemon juice and lemon bitters to an ice-filled cocktail shaker.

2. Shake it all about until the mixture is frosty and divide into 2 champagne flutes.

3. Top with tonic water until it reaches around 75% full.

4. Garnish with rock candy sticks and serve.

Ginger Peach Bellini

Fiery ginger and sweet peaches marry together to form the perfect partnership.

Servings: 4-6

Total Time: 5mins

Ingredients:

- 3 ripe peaches (peeled, pitted. chopped)
- ½" piece fresh ginger (peeled, chopped)
- 1 tsp caster sugar
- 1 Bottle of alcohol-free sparkling wine

Directions:

1. Put the peaches and ginger in a food blender and process until silky smooth.

2. Add the sugar, mix to combine and taste. Add a little more sugar if necessary.

3. Pour 2 tablespoons of the peach puree into champagne flutes and slowly fill each glass to the top with alcohol-free wine.

Holiday Sunrise

A bright and colorful vacation mocktail to bring back memories of sea and sand.

Servings: 1

Total Time: 2mins

Ingredients:

- ¼ cup fresh orange juice
- ½ cup lemonade
- 2 tsp grenadine
- Cherry (to garnish)

Directions:

1. Add the fresh orange juice and lemonade to a glass.

2. Next, add 2 teaspoons of grenadine. Stir.

3. Garnish with a cherry and serve.

Mock Champagne

Serve this virgin champagne to your dinner party guests, and they are sure to come back for more.

Servings: 6

Total Time: 3mins

Ingredients:

- 1 quart ginger ale
- 1 quart white grape juice
- 1 quart pineapple juice
- Ice
- Fruit slice (to garnish)

Directions:

1. In a large pitcher or jug combine the first 3 ingredients and stir well to incorporate. Add the ice and stir.

2. Garnish with a fruit slice of choice.

Raspberry Pomegranate Sherbet Fizz

Taste the rainbow with this fruitylicious cocktail bursting with berries, melon, and citrus.

Servings: 1

Total Time: 5mins

Ingredients:

- 4 tbsp. pomegranate juice
- 4-6 small scoops raspberry sherbet
- 2 tbsp. pomegranate arils
- Sparkling non-alcoholic apple cider

Directions:

1. Pour the juice into a large cocktail glass.

2. Alternate scoops of sherbet with a sprinkling of pomegranate arils until the glass is filled to the top.

3. Finish with a glug of alcohol free apple cider and serve!

Red Apple Delight

The flavor of a crisp red apple in a glass.

Servings: 4

Total Time: 10mins

Ingredients:

- 1½ cups red apple juice
- ¾ cup sweetened lime juice
- 4 tsp grenadine
- 1 cup ice (crushed)
- ¼ cup soda water

Directions:

1. Add the apple and lime juice along with the grenadine into a cocktail mixer. Shake well.

2. Fill 4 martini glasses with crushed ice and strain the cocktail equally into the glasses.

3. Finish each with a dash of soda water. Stir each gently with a long spoon and serve.

Roy Rogers

A simple but classic mocktail perfect for little ones.

Servings: 1

Total Time: 2mins

Ingredients:

- ¼ ounce grenadine
- 8 ounce cola
- 1-2 maraschino cherries (for topping)

Directions:

1. Add the grenadine and cola into a tall glass. Stir well with a tall spoon and top with plenty of ice.

2. Top with cherries and serve!

Sweet Cherry Lime Cooler

Tart zesty lime juice and soda is sweetened with fresh cherries and organic honey for a refreshing mocktail perfect for those hot summer afternoons.

Servings: 1

Total Time: 5mins

Ingredients:

- 12 sweet cherries (pitted)
- 2 tsp organic honey
- ¼ cup cranberry juice
- 2 tbsp. freshly squeezed lime juice
- Dash sparkling water
- Dash lemon and lime flavored soda

Directions:

1. Add the cherries and honey into a cocktail mixer. Muddle well and pour over the cranberry and lime juice. Toss in plenty of ice and shake well for 45-60 seconds.

2. Strain into a large cocktail glass. Top with ice and finish with a dash of sparkling water and soda.

The Rainbow

Taste the rainbow with this fruitylicious cocktail bursting with berries, melon, and citrus.

Servings: 1

Total Time: 5mins

Ingredients:

- 3 fresh raspberries
- 5 fresh blueberries
- 2 medium chunks seedless watermelon
- 2 small dashes Angostura bitters
- 2 tbsp. freshly squeezed orange juice
- Crushed ice
- 3 tbsp. ginger ale

Directions:

1. Add the first 3 ingredients into the bottom of a large glass. Muddle well and pour over the bitters and juice. Stir gently with a long spoon. Top off with crushed ice and finish with a dash of ginger ale.

Watermelon Slushie

Kids love watermelon, and this three-ingredient mocktail is sure to be a firm favorite.

Servings: 1

Total Time: 8hours 5mins

Ingredients:

- 1 small watermelon (peeled, seeded, cubed)
- 2½ cups almond milk
- Sprig of fresh mint

Directions:

1. Place the watermelon chunks in the freezer overnight.

2. When the watermelon is fully frozen, using a food blender; blitz the watermelon along with the almond milk until a silky smooth consistency.

3. Pour the drink into a tall glass and garnish with a sprig of mint.

Herbs and Flowers

Blood Orange Rosemary Spritzer

Fragrant rosemary complements the bittersweetness of blood orange beautifully.

Servings: 1

Total Time: 30mins

Ingredients:

Rosemary syrup:

- 1 cup cold water
- 1 cup sugar
- 3 sprigs rosemary

Mocktail:

- 2 tbsp. orange dry soda
- 2 tbsp. freshly squeezed blood orange juice
- 2 tsp homemade rosemary syrup
- Ice
- 4 tbsp. sparkling mineral water

Directions:

1. First make the rosemary syrup, using a small saucepan combine the water, sugar, and rosemary. Over medium heat, while occasionally stirring bring to boil. The syrup is ready when all of the sugar has dissolved.

2. Remove the syrup from the heat and put to one side for 8-10 minutes.

3. Strain, discard the rosemary sprigs and transfer to a jar to completely cool.

4. Add the orange soda, along with the orange juice and cooled rosemary syrup to a tall glass and fill with ice to around 2/3 full.

5. Fill the glass with mineral water.

Blueberry Mojito Mocktail

This mojito is bursting with berries.

Servings: 2

Total Time: 3mins

Ingredients:

- 1 cup blueberries
- 10 fresh mint leaves
- 2 tsp white sugar
- Freshly squeezed juice of 2 limes
- Ice (crushed)
- Sparkling water
- Wedge of lime

Directions:

1. Add the blueberries to a food blender and puree. Put to one side.

2. In a cocktail shaker muddle, the mint leaves along with the sugar.

3. Next, add the lime juice and pureed berries. Shake it all about.

4. Pour the mixture into 2 Collins glasses and fill to the top with crushed ice.

5. Fill the glasses with sparkling water and stir.

6. Garnish with a wedge of lime.

Ginger, Basil, and Grapefruit Mimosas

A sharing mimosa mocktail to get your party or gathering off to a flying start.

Servings: 4-6

Total Time: 2hours 35mins

Ingredients:

Basil Syrup:

- 1 cup sugar
- 1 cup water
- 1 cup loosely packed fresh basil
- 2 cups of ice
- 3 (12 ounce) cans of ginger soda
- Juice of 1 large grapefruit
- ¼ cup basil simple syrup
- Grapefruit segments (to garnish)

Directions:

1. To make the syrup, add the sugar and cold water to a small saucepan and over medium heat while stirring heat until the sugar is dissolved; this will take around 2-3 minutes. Add the fresh basil and allow to steep for 18-20 minutes. Strain the syrup and discard the basil.

2. Transfer the syrup to a jar, cover, and chill in the refrigerator for 2 hours (you can store the syrup for up to 21 days).

3. Fill a pitcher or jug half way to the top with ice and add the soda, grapefruit juice, and syrup. Stir to combine.

4. Garnish with grapefruit segments.

Ginger Beer Mock Mojito

Ginger beer combines with lime and mint in this zesty mock mojito

Servings: 1

Total Time: 1mins

Ingredients:

- 10 mint leaves
- 2 ounces fresh lime juice
- Ice
- 4 ounces ginger beer
- Lime wedges (to garnish)

Directions:

1. In a tall glass, muddle the mint leaves along with the lime juice. Add 2-3 cubes of ice and pour in the ginger beer.

2. Garnish with a wedge of lime.

Grapefruit Sage Mocktail

Sharp grapefruit and savory sage come together in the perfect pairing to make a hydrating drink.

Servings: 2

Total Time: 3mins

Ingredients:

- 1 cup ice
- 4 sage leaves
- 1 cup fresh grapefruit juice
- Salt (for rimming)

Directions:

1. In a cocktail shaker combine the ice along with the sage leaves and fresh grapefruit juice. Shake it all about to infuse the flavors.

2. Rim the glasses with salt and pour in the mocktail.

3. Enjoy!

Honey Sage Soda

Sweet honey combines with the savory flavor of sage to make this ginger-infused mocktail. Serve this soda in a mason jar for a real taste of the South.

Servings: 2

Total Time: 1hour 10mins

Ingredients:

Honey sage simple syrup:*

- 1 cup water
- ½ cup honey
- 3 sage leaves

For the soda:

- 2 tbsp. honey sage simple syrup
- 1 slice fresh lime (squeezed)
- Ginger ale
- 3 sage leaves (to garnish)

Directions:

1. First, make the syrup. In a saucepan over high heat, bring the cold water along with the honey and sage leaves to boil. Reduce the heat and simmer for 2 minutes. Turn the heat off, strain, discard the sage and allow the syrup to cool.

2. Once the syrup is cool, it is ready to use.

3. To make the mocktail take 2 tall glasses, add the simple syrup to the lime juice and fill with ginger ale. Top with lots of ice and garnish with a sage leaf.

*The syrup can be stored in the refrigerator in a sealed container for 5-7 days. This recipe makes sufficient syrup for 2-3 drinks.

Juicy Julep

A non-alcoholic version of the classic cocktail that has been around since the 18th century.

Servings: 1

Total Time: 3mins

Ingredients:

- Ice
- 1½ ounces orange juice
- 1½ ounces pineapple juice
- 1½ ounces freshly squeeze lime juice
- Ginger ale
- 1 tsp mint (finely chopped)
- Sprig of mint (to garnish)
- Lime wedge (to garnish)

Directions:

1. Add ice to a Collins glass and pour in the orange juice, pineapple juice, and lime juice.

2. Fill to the very top with ginger ale and stir in the chopped mint.

3. Garnish with a mint sprig and wedge of lime.

4. Serve.

Lady Lavender Mocktail*

A luxurious and surprising alcohol-free drink for ladies who lunch.

Servings: 1

Total Time: 1hour 20mins

Ingredients:

Lavender syrup:

- ½ cup cold water
- ½ cup sugar
- 1 tbsp. dried lavender

For the mocktail:

- ¼ cup fresh lemon juice
- 1½ tbsp. lavender simple syrup
- ¼ tsp grenadine
- 3 dashes non-alcoholic bitters
- Lavender sprig (to garnish)

Directions:

1. To make the syrup; combine the cold water along with the sugar and dried lavender in a small saucepan and bring to boil. When the mixture is boiling, remove the pan from the heat and allow to cool. When the syrup is cooled using a fine mesh sieve remove the lavender.

2. To make the mocktail; using a cocktail shaker filled with ice combine the first 4 mocktail ingredients (lemon juice through bitters) and shake it all about.

3. Strain the liquid into a glass and garnish with a sprig of lavender

*You can always add a drop of purple or blue food coloring to the mocktail if you wish.

Lemon Basil Daiquiri Slushie

A bright mocktail slushie to make in minutes.

Servings: 1

Total Time: 2mins

Ingredients:

- 4 basil leaves
- Juice of 1 large lemon
- 1 tbsp. sugar
- 1 tbsp. water
- Ice cubes

Directions:

1. Combine all of the ingredients in a food blender and, on high-speed blend until silky smooth. Add more ice if needed.

2. Enjoy.

Peach, Berry and Thyme Melba

A light fizzy drink that tastes just like a Peach Melba dessert, if not better

Servings: 8

Total Time: 4hours 35mins

Ingredients:

- 1 cup granulated sugar
- 1 cup cold water
- 1 medium, ripe peach (halved, pitted, cut into 1/8" sliced)
- ½ pint fresh raspberries
- 30 sprigs fresh lemon thyme (rinsed, woody ends trimmed)
- 1 quart club soda (cold)
- Ice

Directions:

1. Over medium to high heat, in a saucepan bring the sugar along with the cold water to simmer, occasionally stirring for 4-5 minutes, or until the sugar is dissolved. Remove the pan from the heat and set aside to cool. When the syrup is room temperature transfer to a container (with lid) and add the slices of peach to the container, stir to combine and seal.

2. Place the sealed container in the refrigerator for a minimum of 4 hours. This will allow the flavors to infuse.

3. When you are ready, pour the syrup through a fine mesh strainer over a mixing bowl and discard the peaches. To the bowl, add a ¼ pint of raspberries and 15 sprigs of thyme. You will need the remaining raspberries and thyme as garnish.

4. Next, using a potato masher, quickly mash until the raspberries release their juices.

5. Rest a large mesh strainer over a large jug and carefully pour in the raspberry mixture. Press lightly on the solids, with a wooden spoon or spatula and discard any solids.

6. Pour in the club soda together with ice and gently stir until incorporated.

7. Using clean hands, very gently bruise the remaining 15 sprigs of thyme. You can do this using your hand to crush the thyme rather than mangling it. Put to one side.

8. Pour the Peach, Berry and Thyme Melba into Collins glasses filled ice.

9. Garnish each drink with fresh raspberries and a sprig or two of crushed thyme.

Pear & Thyme Spritzer

Thyme has a pleasantly mild flavor, but when making drinks, you should always use fresh, rather than dried thyme. This mocktail is the perfect 'pear-ing' of fresh ingredients.

Servings: 1

Total Time: 2hours 10mins

Ingredients:

Thyme syrup:

- 1 cup water
- 1 cup sugar
- 6 sprigs thyme

For the Spritzer:

- 2 tbsp. pear puree
- ½ tbsp. fresh lemon juice
- 2 tbsp. orange dry
- 1 tsp thyme simple syrup
- Crushed ice
- Sparkling mineral water
- Sprig of thyme (to garnish)
- Slice of pear (to garnish)

Directions:

1. First, make the thyme syrup by combine the cup of water and sugar with the thyme sprigs in a small saucepan over medium heat. Bring the mixture to boil, while occasionally stirring, until the sugar has dissolved.

2. Remove the pan from the heat and put to one side to allow the ingredients to infuse, for 10 minutes.

3. Using a fine mesh strainer, strain the syrup and discard the thyme. Pour into a jar with a lid and allow the syrup to completely cool.

4. Next, combine the pear puree along with the fresh lemon juice, orange dry, and 1 teaspoon of thyme syrup in a tall glass. Fill the glass with crushed ice to around 75% full and fill to the top with sparkling water.

5. Garnish with a sprig of thyme and a slice of pear.

Rose and Elderflower Mocktail

A real show-stopping light and refreshing drink.

Servings: 1

Total Time: 3hours 5mins

Ingredients:

- 12 perfect rose petals
- ½ tsp rosewater
- 1 (9ounce) bottle Wild English Elderflower

Directions:

1. First, make ice cubes. Half fill an ice cube tray with cold water and place a rose petal inside each cube. Transfer to the refrigerator 60-90 minutes, or until the petal is securely set in the water. Fill the cubes with water and freeze until set.

2. Fill a tall glass with rose ice cubes and pour in the rosewater.

3. Top with sparkling elderflower.

Rosemary Pear Mocktail Spritzer

It's time to add some sparkle to your life with the perfect marriage of rosemary and pears in this marvellous mocktail.

Servings: 4

Total Time: 1hour

Ingredients:

Rosemary simple syrup:

- 1 cup cold water
- 1 cup sugar
- 8 sprigs of rosemary

For the Spritzer:

- 4 cups pear juice
- ¾ cup rosemary simple syrup
- 2 tbsp. lemon juice (freshly squeezed)
- Seltzer
- Rosemary sprigs (for garnish)

Directions:

1. First, make the syrup by combine the cold water and sugar in a small saucepan and bring to boil. Add the sprigs of rosemary and stir well until the sugar is dissolved.

2. Remove the pan from the heat and allow to rest for 40 minutes.

3. Strain the syrup through a fine mesh strainer and discard the rosemary and put to one side until completely cool.

4. To make the spritzer, add the pear juice along with the cooled rosemary syrup and lemon juice. Stir well until combined.

5. Fill the glasses with ice and divide the mixture evenly between the 4 glasses, to approximately half full.

6. Top with seltzer and garnish with rosemary.

Sin Free Sangria

Lots of fresh fruit combined with ginger ale and apple cider – who needs alcohol!

Servings: 1

Total Time: 2mins

Ingredients:

- I medium apple (finely sliced)
- 1 cup raspberries (chopped)
- 1 cup blueberries (chopped)
- 1 can club soda
- 1 regular can ginger ale (chilled)
- Non-alcoholic apple cider

Directions:

1. In a large pitcher or jug, combine the fruit.

2. Next, pour in the club soda and ginger ale.

3. Finally, add the apple cider and stir.

Author's Afterthoughts

Thanks ever so much to each of my cherished readers for investing the time to read this book!

I know you could have picked from many other books but you chose this one. So a big thanks for downloading this book and reading all the way to the end.

If you enjoyed this book or received value from it, I'd like to ask you for a favor. Please take a few minutes to post an honest and heartfelt review on Amazon.com. Your support does make a difference and helps to benefit other people.

Thanks!

Daniel Humphreys

About the Author

Daniel Humphreys

Many people will ask me if I am German or Norman, and my answer is that I am 100% unique! Joking aside, I owe my cooking influence mainly to my mother who was British! I can certainly make a mean Sheppard's pie, but when it comes to preparing Bratwurst sausages and drinking beer with friends, I am also all in!

I am taking you on this culinary journey with me and hope you can appreciate my diversified background. In my 15 years career as a chef, I never had a dish returned to me by one of clients, so that should say something about me! Actually, I will take that back. My worst critic is my four years old son, who refuses to taste anything that is green color. That shall pass, I am sure.

My hope is to help my children discover the joy of cooking and sharing their creations with their loved ones, like I did all my life. When you develop a passion for cooking and my suspicious is that you have one as well, it usually sticks for life. The best advice I can give anyone as a professional chef is invest. Invest your time, your heart in each meal you are creating. Invest also a little money in good cooking hardware and quality ingredients. But most of all enjoy every meal you prepare with YOUR friends and family!

Printed in Great Britain
by Amazon